Natural Phenomena in Greek Mythology

Don Nardo

San Diego, CA

© 2017 ReferencePoint Press, Inc.
Printed in the United States

For more information, contact:
ReferencePoint Press, Inc.
PO Box 27779
San Diego, CA 92198
www.ReferencePointPress.com

LIBRARY OF CONGRESS CATALOGING-IN-PUBLICATION DATA

Names: Nardo, Don, 1947- author.
Title: Natural phenomena in Greek mythology / by Don Nardo.
Description: San Diego : ReferencePoint Press, 2017. | Series: The Library of
  Greek mythology series | Includes bibliographical references and index.
Identifiers: LCCN 2015048353 (print) | LCCN 2016006664 (ebook) | ISBN
  9781601529725 (hardback) | ISBN 9781601529732 (epub)
Subjects: LCSH: Creation. | Nature. | Mythology, Greek.
Classification: LCC BL795.C68 N375 2017 (print) | LCC BL795.C68 (ebook) | DDC
  398.20938/06--dc23
LC record available at http://lccn.loc.gov/2015048353

Contents

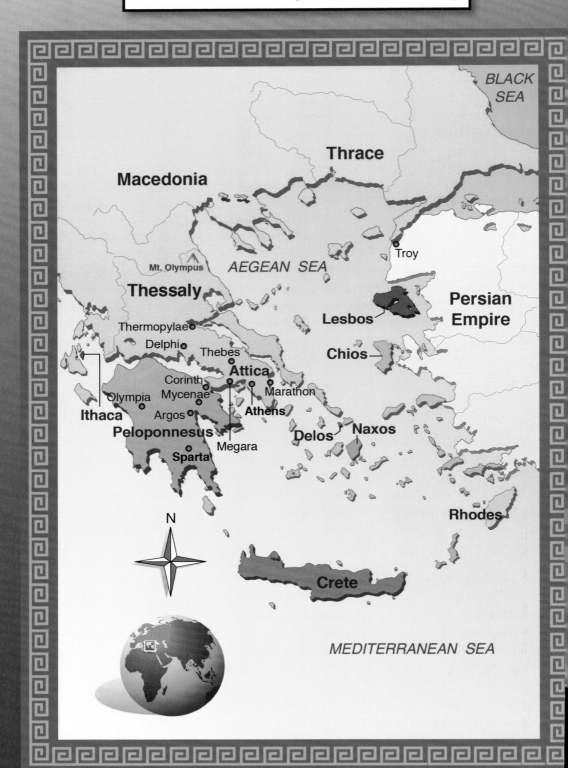

Ancient Greece (Circa 500 BCE)

BLACK SEA

Thrace

Macedonia

AEGEAN SEA

Troy

Mt. Olympus

Thessaly

Lesbos

Persian Empire

Thermopylae

Delphi

Chios

Thebes

Attica

Corinth

Marathon

Olympia

Mycenae

Athens

Ithaca

Argos

Peloponnesus

Delos

Naxos

Megara

Sparta

N

Rhodes

Crete

MEDITERRANEAN SEA

Introduction

The Origins of Nature's Wonders

The great gleaming face of the sun god Helios stared down at the son he had sired with a mortal woman named Clymene. That youth, Phaethon, now in his late teens, was visiting his divine father, who each day drove his luminous chariot across the sky. Just for one day, Phaethon explained, he would like to be allowed to pilot that shining vehicle.

As the first-century-BCE Roman storyteller Ovid recalled, "Grief and remorse flooded his father's soul, and bitterly he shook his glorious head." It would be far too dangerous for an inexperienced boy to lead such a hugely energetic team of horses, Helios explained. "You seek a privilege that ill befits your growing years." It was a privilege "to which even the gods may not aspire," the sun god said. Indeed, "even he whose hand hurls thunderbolts," that is, the mighty Zeus, leader of the gods, "may never drive my team."[1]

Yet the impulsive young man refused to take *no* for an answer. He kept insisting over and over that he was strong and mature enough to handle Helios's chariot and steeds. Finally, the father's will wore thin, and he reluctantly agreed to let his son have his way. Soon after that, Phaethon climbed atop the glittering vehicle and drove it upward into the sky.

It did not take long, however, for just the sort of trouble that Helios had feared to occur. "The chariot, lacking now its usual load," Ovid wrote, bounced back and forth, and the alarmed horses "ran wild and left the well-worn highway. Phaethon, dazed with fear, could neither use the reins nor find the road." The surprised young man glanced downward and saw all of Greece, along with neighboring lands and entire continents spreading out from horizon to horizon. A wave of dizziness swept over him, "his face grew pale, his knees in sudden fear shook, and his eyes were blind with light so bright."[2]

The stampeding stallions swerved and swayed from side to side and galloped through airy regions unfamiliar to them. "Out of control," in Ovid's words, they "ran amok amid the stars fixed in the vault of heaven, hurtling the chariot where no road had run."[3] In one instant they yanked the chariot upward to heaven's heights, then suddenly plunged downward at breakneck speed toward Earth's surface.

Meanwhile, Helios's sister, the moon goddess Selene, watched in horror as the vehicle's extreme heat caused "scalding clouds of steam" to form and "the parched fields to crack deep."[4] Vast mountain forests burst into flames, and entire cities were burnt to ashes in mere seconds. The great Helios himself stood aghast at and helpless to stop the mayhem his now terrified son was creating. The worried god wondered if the entire world would be destroyed.

Quaint, Cherished Stories

Although at that moment in Phaethon's rousing tale the sun god had no idea what would happen next, from a young age all classical Greeks knew the ending of that story well. The term *classical Greeks* was coined by modern scholars. When used in a very general way, it designates the inhabitants of the Greek-speaking world from around 700 to 300 BCE. That was the period in which the Greeks lived primarily in city-states, tiny nations each made up of a central town surrounded and supported by nearby villages and farms. It was also the era in which Greece, particularly the state of Athens between 500 and 400 BCE, created a burst of magnificent literature, art, and democratic ideals. That splendid cultural legacy went on to impress and inspire all later generations of Western, or European-based, civilization.

> ## WORD ORIGINS
>
> ### myth
>
> In modern life: a traditional story usually containing fictional characters and events from a past era.
>
> In ancient Greece: *muthos*, meaning an ancient story.

Phaethon begged his father, the sun god Helios, to be allowed to drive his father's chariot across the sky for one day. But the inexperienced Phaethon was unable to control the horses, and the chariot plunged toward the ground.

The residents of classical Greece inherited and treasured a large collection of stories from their past, each of which they called a *muthos*, or myth. Like many other aspects of ancient Greek culture, most of those tales survived the ages to the present day. A hefty proportion of them, including the one about the impetuous young risk taker Phaethon, deal with various kinds of natural phenomena. The story of Helios and his half-mortal son covers two such aspects of nature. One—the sun god's journey across the sky in his dazzling chariot—provided the ancient Greeks with an explanation of the sun's daily movements from one horizon to the other. The other natural occurrence described in the myth is an earthly disaster brought about by an excess of solar heat.

Hundreds of other surviving Greek myths deal in one way or another with natural phenomena. Indeed, classical scholar Adrienne Mayor remarks, "Greek myth is a complex skein [knotted thread] of tales about the origin of the natural world and the history of its inhabitants."[5] Some of these tales tell how various other objects in the heavens supposedly came to be and operated on a daily or yearly basis. These include the moon, planets, stars, and Milky Way. Other myths deal with weather phenomena of diverse kinds—among them storms, rainbows, thunder, and lightning. The Greeks thought that each of these things was caused or guided by one or more gods. The same was true for various natural disasters, such as earthquakes, floods, and volcanic eruptions, all described in multiple myths. Still other natural phenomena inhabiting the quaint stories the ancient Greeks so greatly cherished recounted the origins of fire, the seasons, humans, and animals.

A Mangled Memory

The early classical Greeks believed that these and other wonders of nature came into being not long before a special and in many ways miraculous era of their dimly remembered past. They called it the "Age of Heroes" because they believed that a number of heroic humans interacted with or were even born of gods in those days. In later years the myths that came from that distant era were not just entertaining tales for children. Instead, they were, at least in part, historical narratives that told how the various aspects of nature came to be.

Historians and other educated modern observers know that those Greek stories about natural phenomena are largely fanciful, rather than strictly historic. Yet a considerable amount of evidence shows that a certain proportion of the myths in question were either based on or inspired by real events and characters. For instance, it is now clear that the so-called Age of Heroes was in many ways a mangled *mneme* (Greek for "memory") of a real prior Greek civilization that the classical Greeks knew nothing about.

That society reached its height about a thousand years before the Athenian cultural renaissance of the fifth century BCE. In what scholars call the late Bronze Age (circa 1600–1150 BCE), mainland Greece and the islands near its shores were home to two culturally advanced peoples. The first, dubbed the Minoans by historians, occupied many of the islands, especially the largest Greek isle, Crete, on the Aegean Sea's southern rim. The mainlanders, meanwhile, are today called the Mycenaeans, after their town of Mycenae, first excavated in the late 1800s.

The two Bronze Age peoples constructed small but powerful kingdoms featuring large stone structures that often tripled as palaces, fortresses, and religious centers. The islanders and mainlanders interacted and traded with each other, as well as with non-Greek cities and kingdoms in the eastern Mediterranean region. Among them were Egypt, parts of what is now Syria, and Troy, in what is now northwestern Turkey. Ultimately, during the years spanning about 1200 to 1100 BCE, the Minoan-Mycenaean civilization utterly collapsed for reasons that are still not completely understood.

WORD ORIGINS

mneme

In ancient Greece: a memory.

In modern life: amnesia, meaning a loss of memory.

Into the Realm of Legend

In the wake of that collapse, the Greek region descended into a culturally backward state during what modern experts call the Dark Age (circa 1150–800 BCE). The palace-centers became deserted and fell into disrepair. At the same time, art, architecture, writing, literature, record keeping, and other signs of high civilization largely disappeared. Such major losses caused Greece's once impressive Bronze Age culture to rapidly slip into the realm of legend. Decade by decade, clear memories of the old kingdoms faded, causing some of their key leaders, warriors, and events to gradually morph into myths.

Not all aspects of these stories were based on fact, however. Some parts of the myths, including those about natural phenomena, were artifacts of good, imaginative storytelling. During the Dark Age and well beyond, storytellers called bards, or rhapsodes (literally "song stitchers"), traveled from village to village. They pieced together and recited narratives of life and events from ages past, at times exaggerating them or even inventing new characters and plot twists. As scholar Philip Mayerson says, many modern experts

believe that behind these heroic legends are specks or motes of historical fact, the residue from a long period of oral transmission. In the course of being handed down from father to son and from bard to bard, the dry data of history, such as political, social, and economic factors, were first eroded and then encrusted with highly imaginative detail until they were turned into the fascinating stories which have survived to this day.[6]

Chapter One

Weather and Natural Disasters

I f a Greek from the early years of the classical period had suddenly stepped through a time portal to the present day, he or she would be quite naturally perplexed and disturbed by many things. That person would certainly be astounded to see meteorologists, or weather experts, predicting rain, snow, or sunny days for the coming week. Moreover, he or she would learn that storms, lightning, and other weather events are naturally occurring phenomena.

The time traveler would probably find that last fact particularly surprising and perhaps troubling. After all, the average early classical Greek was brought up to believe that Zeus, Poseidon, and other gods controlled the weather. The proof for that was a group of myths that explained the origins and workings of natural phenomena, including weather-related ones. According to one modern expert, "Ancient Greek mythology is an example of how early civilizations tried to explain the then unexplainable forces of nature." Most often they did so by imagining those forces to be the handiwork of various divine beings. Indeed, "many ancient Greek gods and goddesses were elements of weather and seasons personified." From that viewpoint, "all occurrences of favorable or poor weather were thought to be a direct result of godly intervention, a constant theme in Greek myth, art, theater and literature."[7]

Such beliefs routinely affected daily life. Only one example was the refusal by most Greeks to bury a person who had died after being struck by lightning. The assumption was that the deceased had angered

Zeus or another deity and that giving the body a proper funeral might irritate the god even more.

Similar beliefs derived from ancient myths shaped the way the early classical Greeks explained natural disasters, some of which were weather related. The Greeks were "just as liable to disaster as we are," writes scholar Stewart Perowne. "And so they, like us, did their best to encompass two things—to ward off disasters that might occur, and to account for those that did. An earthquake—was it about to happen?" In the modern world, "we have seismological stations. The Greeks had gods and heroes. The result was exactly the same. The earthquake happened. With us, it is a disaster to be explained; and so it was for them." But instead of a scientific explanation, "the Greeks had an enthralling story—a myth. In fact, Zeus was angry. Or Hera was jealous. So Poseidon, the earth-shaker, got to work."[8]

Lord of Lightning and Thunder

The Greeks called the deities in charge of the weather the *theoi meteoroi*, literally the "weather gods." Those beings were led by Zeus, who was also widely acknowledged as the leader of all existing gods. "Father Zeus," as people often called him, had direct control of weather effects such as rain, thunder (*bronte*), and lightning, which the Greeks also called thunderbolts. Those brilliant, potent flashes of what is now known to be electrical energy were Zeus's principal trademark, or symbol. Greek writers, including the great eighth-century-BCE epic poet Homer, frequently described him as the "thunder maker," the "cloud gatherer," and so forth.

It was thought that Zeus sometimes displayed storm clouds and lightning flashes mainly to show off his enormous power and keep humans in line. But just as often he employed his thunderbolts as weapons, and the Greek myths are full of examples. One of that god's earliest military victories, for instance, witnessed his repeated use of lightning to fend off the enemy—an army of giants bent on destroying Zeus and his fellow gods.

> ## WORD ORIGINS
>
> ### *bronte*
>
> In ancient Greece: thunder.
>
> In modern life: Brontosaurus, a dinosaur whose name means "thunder lizard."

Zeus, leader of the gods, controlled rain, thunder, and lightning and often used thunderbolts as weapons. In one myth, he threw thunderbolts to vanquish an enemy army in an epic battle called the Gigantomachy.

According to the second-century-CE Greek myth-teller now known as Pseudo-Apollodorus, "These creatures were unsurpassed in the size of their bodies and unconquerable by virtue of their power. They were frightening in appearance, with long hair that swept down from their heads and chins, and serpent-scales covering their lower limbs, [and they hurled] rocks and flaming oak trees at the sky."[9]

The battle, which the Greeks called the Gigantomachy, raged for days. Finally, after Apollo, Athena, and other deities had slain or incapacitated the strongest giants, Pseudo-Apollodorus went on, "Zeus destroyed the rest by throwing his thunderbolts."[10] Classical Greeks familiar with this and similar myths were naturally

Myth-Tellers' Corner: Homer

Homer's birthplace and birth date were unknown even to the now famous classical Greeks in the fifth and fourth centuries BCE. (Most modern
scholars who specialize in Homer and his works think he was born on the
Aegean island of Chios sometime in the 700s BCE.) But the fact that these
and other details of his life were uncertain to later ancient Greeks did not
diminish his importance to them. As one of the better Homeric translators,
Richmond Lattimore, puts it, for the Greeks, Homer "stood at the head of
their literary tradition. All knew him and few challenged his greatness."

The man whom most classical Greeks referred to simply as "the poet"
was one of a series of traveling minstrels called bards, who both composed and recited lengthy tales in flowing, appealing verse. Homer seems
to have created the final versions of two of these majestic works, which
earlier bards had recited, embellished, and handed down to him. Of these
epics, in Lattimore's words, "the *Iliad* deals with the story of Troy, the *Odyssey* with the homecoming of the Greek heroes after the capture of the
city; in particular, the homecoming of Odysseus, the adventures, temp-
tations, and dangers he went through before he made his way back to
Ithaca," the island kingdom he ruled. Lattimore and other modern scholars emphasize that the two Homeric epics exerted a major influence on
Greek society, customs, and ideas throughout the ancient era.

Quoted in Richmond Lattimore, trans., *The Iliad of Homer*. Chicago: University of Chicago Press, 1963,
pp. 13–14.

impressed, and someone composed a hymn that addressed and honored Zeus's role as the hurler of thunderbolts. That work reads in
part, "To Zeus, lightning-maker. I call the mighty, holy, splendid,
light, aerial, dreadful-sounding, fiery-bright, flaming, ethereal light,
with angry voice, lighting through lucid clouds with crashing noise.
Untamed, to whom resentments dire belong, pure, holy power, all-

parent, great and strong. Come, and benevolent these rites attend, and grant the mortal life a pleasing end."[11]

Also inspired by the myths depicting Zeus as a weather god, some unknown Greek honored Zeus with a hymn citing his role as thunder maker. "It is yours to brandish thunders strong and dire," the work states in part. That powerful being's sudden bolt of thunder "can raise the hair upright," and such deafening thunderclaps "shake the heart of humans with wild affright. Sudden, unconquered, holy, thundering god, with noise unbounded flying all abroad. With all-devouring force, entire and strong, horrid, untamed, [earth] trembles at your ire. The sea all-shining and each beast that hears the sound terrific, with dread horror fears."[12]

The Wind Gods Intervene?

Numerous Greek myths also addressed another common weather phenomenon—the winds. The chief wind god, who appears in several of those stories, was Aeolus, who was said to dwell on a remote and very unusual island. In his great epic the *Odyssey*, Homer had the hero Odysseus say, "His island floats in the air. It features a very strong bronze wall running around it, with a rocky cliff looming above."[13]

Odysseus and his men, who were wandering the seas and searching for a way to get back to their homeland of Ithaca, pleaded with the god to help them. "He was willing to aid us," Odysseus recalled. "He gave me a bag made of the hide of his own ox and inside he stuffed the winds from all around the area. Aeolus put the bag on my ship and tied it shut with a shiny silver string, making sure that not a single breath of air could escape."[14] The one exception was the west wind, which Aeolus commanded to blow Odysseus's fleet toward home. Unfortunately for these wayward Greeks, however, a few of Odysseus's crew later unwisely tampered with the bag, which caused it to fly open. A stormlike mass of speeding *aer* (Greek for "air") suddenly rushed out and blew the vessels away from Ithaca instead of toward it.

WORD ORIGINS

aer

In ancient Greece: air.

In modern life: aerospace, the industry that puts rockets and astronauts into the region beyond Earth's atmosphere, or "air."

Aeolus was not the god of *all* winds in the Greek myths. Instead, he was in charge of several deities who each specialized in a particular kind of wind or specific wind direction. Boreas, for example, was the god who controlled the north wind, along with the cold winter winds. Zephyros brought the west wind and the pleasant breezes of springtime; the south wind and summer storms were the work of Notos; and the weather deity Euros was in charge of the east wind.

The classical Greeks enjoyed hearing the old stories about the various gods of the winds, especially the incident involving Aeolus and his bag of breezes from Homer's *Odyssey*. But the Greeks did not see such tales merely as casual entertainment. Evidence shows that they believed those gods, and weather deities in general, sometimes intervened in human affairs. Just such an event occurred during the Greco-Persian wars of the fifth century BCE. In 492 BCE a large fleet of Persian warships tried to invade Greece by sailing around Mount Athos, in the northern Aegean region. But as the Greek historian Herodotus, who was born shortly after the incident, wrote, the vessels "were caught by a violent northerly gale, which proved too much for the ships to cope with. A great many of them were driven ashore and wrecked on Athos."[15] Most Greeks were convinced that this was no random happening, but that one or more deities had conspired to halt the invasion and save Greece.

There was also agreement among many classical Greeks that a wind god became involved in the fate of the famous Athenian philosopher Socrates. Athenian officials came to see him as a troublemaker and wanted to get rid of him. So in 399 BCE they trumped up some charges, including that he had corrupted young people with his ideas. In the trial, the jury sentenced Socrates to death.

But a ship had recently been sent on a sacred religious mission to an Aegean island, and it was against Athenian law to hold an execution until it returned. So the condemned philosopher sat in jail waiting for the vessel, which was weeks overdue thanks to some unusual winds that made sailing unsafe. To the Greeks, scholar Clinton Corcoran

Odysseus asked the wind god Aeolus to help him and his men get back home, so Aeolus gave him a bag stuffed with all the winds except the west wind, which he commanded to blow Odysseus's fleet home.

points out, "the delay of the execution because of contrary winds" was widely seen as a case of divine intervention into Socrates's life. Many people interpreted it as "an expression of the gods' anger with his execution, or a desire on the part of the gods to delay [his] execution."[16]

Earthquakes and Volcanoes

Just as the gods of the winds were thought to interfere in earthly affairs, other gods in the Greek myths caused disasters that supposedly affected human society. Poseidon was a classic example. Although he was the principal sea god, he was also thought to cause earthquakes, often by jabbing at the ground with his signature weapon and chief symbol, his trident (three-pronged spear).

The early classical Greeks also connected other immortal beings mentioned in myths, including Enceladus, to earthquakes. That unsavory character was one of the giants who fought against Zeus and his divine followers in the Gigantomachy. Athena, goddess of wisdom and war, was said to have thrown the island of Sicily on top of Enceladus. Thereafter, both the Greeks and Romans claimed that he lay trapped beneath the island forever and that when he occasionally squirmed in hopes of escaping, the ground trembled, shaking towns and farms.

Enceladus was also said to cause volcanic eruptions when he yelled threats or exhaled his heavy, hot, and heinous breath. According to the third-century-CE Greek writer Philostratus the Elder, after Athena buried Enceladus beneath Sicily, he refused to surrender: "From beneath the earth he renews the fight and breathes forth this [volcanic] fire as he utters threats."[17]

Most volcanic eruptions, however, were thought to be the work of Hephaestos, the god of the forge and patron and protector of blacksmiths and craftsmen who worked with metals. Some myths described him working in a vast underground workshop with numerous bellows that operated on his vocal commands. The common belief was that when most or all of them were working at one time, they produced an enormous volume of fire and smoke, which blasted upward and took the form of a volcanic eruption.

During classical times and beyond, Greek and Roman writers mentioned several volcanoes they believed to harbor Hephaestos, his forges, and his assistants. But these things were chiefly associated with Mount Etna in Sicily, the most active volcano in Europe both then and now. However, people came to believe that during the years between the major eruptions that Hephaestos caused it was safe enough to climb and explore the mountain. The noted first-century-BCE Greek traveler Strabo described lookouts, huts with cots for sleeping,

"The Sky Explodes"

Here, from his epic poem *The Aeneid*, the Roman writer Virgil describes the god Aeolus employing the winds to batter the fleet commanded by the Trojan hero Aeneas.

Pointing his spear at the hollow mountain, pushed at its flank, [Aeolus musters] the Winds, as it were in a solid mass, [which] hurl themselves through the gates and sweep the land with tornadoes. They have fallen upon the sea, they are heaving it up from its deepest abysses, the whole sea—East wind, South, Sou-wester thick with squalls, [and] all of a sudden the Storm-clouds are snatching the heavens, the daylight from the eyes of the Trojans; night, black night is fallen on the sea. The welkin [sky] explodes, the firmament flickers with thick-and-fast lightning, and everything is threatening the instant death of men. [Indeed] even as [the sailors] cried out [in fear], a howling gust from the North hit the front of the sail, and a wave climbed the sky. Oars snapped; then the ship yawed, wallowing broadside on to the seas: and then, piled up there, a precipice [towering cliff] of sea hung. One vessel was poised on a wave crest; for another the waters, collapsing, showed sea-bottom in the trough: the tide-race boiled with sand. Three times did the South wind spin them towards an ambush of rocks, [and to the sandbar], a piteous spectacle— hammering them on the shallows and hemming them round with sandbanks.

Virgil, *The Aeneid,* trans. Cecil Day-Lewis, excerpted in Theoi Greek Mythology, "Aiolos." www.theoi.com.

Hephaestos, the god of the forge, was believed to be responsible for most volcanic eruptions, especially those from Mount Etna (pictured). He and his assistants worked underground with numerous bellows that produced fire and smoke that blasted upward through volcanoes.

and other facilities for hikers and climbers on Etna's slopes. Near the base of the mountain, he wrote, was

> a small village called Etna, which takes in climbers and sends them on their way, for the ridge of the mountain begins here. Those who had recently climbed to the summit told me that at the top was a level plain [inside the volcanic crater]. Two of their party were courageous enough to venture into that plain, but since the sand on which they were walking was becoming hotter and deeper, they turned back.[18]

Destructive Floods

Floods were also common in the ancient Greco-Roman world, as well as in the Greek myths. Although the chief deity, Zeus, was most often responsible for sending floods to drown people, he was frequently aided by other gods. For example, when human folly angered him, he sometimes ordered Notos, master of summer storms, to soak various regions with torrential rains. Zeus was also known to call on his brother, Poseidon, to generate tsunamis that overflowed onto inland plains.

According to a famous myth, one of Zeus's best-known floods resulted from an experiment he undertook along with his divine messenger, Hermes. The two gods disguised themselves as humble beggars for the purpose of testing the hospitality of the residents of a large valley in Phrygia (in what is now central Turkey). The supposed beggars walked from house to house, including many owned by well-to-do folk, politely asking for a few morsels of food and somewhere—even a stable—to sleep. To Zeus and Hermes's dismay, however, one homeowner after another rudely insulted them and told them to get off their property.

After being rebuffed this way at more than a thousand homes, the disguised deities came to a tiny, ramshackle hut made of straw, tree branches, and river reeds. This time they were greeted by an elderly man and his wife, who introduced themselves as Baucis and Philemon. The couple, who were clearly desperately poor, went out of their way to make the visitors comfortable, including making a dinner from radishes, olives, cabbage, and other inexpensive foodstuffs they had grown near the hut.

While the four diners ate the simple but ample meal, Baucis and Philemon began to notice something odd. Each time their serving plate was almost empty, it suddenly got full again, and their small jug of wine never seemed to grow empty, no matter how many cups they poured from it. Worried they might be the victims of some sort of evil magic, the couple became fearful and started praying to Zeus for help.

Their prayer was answered rather quickly, as Zeus and Hermes suddenly threw off their beggars' outfits and revealed their magnificent true forms to the astounded couple. Taking Baucis and Philemon to a nearby mountaintop, the gods told them not to be afraid. Zeus then gave orders to Poseidon and some other sea gods to unleash a monstrous flood into the valley, a deluge that destroyed all the old couple's neighbors. The only structure spared in the catastrophe was Baucis and Philemon's hut, which Zeus himself changed into a splendid mansion.

Moral Lessons

The classical Greeks plainly recognized that this terrible flood was not the only important theme of the story. A large number of Greek myths, among them many of those involving natural phenomena, contained moral lessons that people took to heart, and the tale of Baucis and Philemon was no exception. The gods killed all of the couple's neighbors for their lack of hospitality and simple human decency.

In fact, extending hospitality to others, including complete strangers—a custom known as *xenia*—was a crucial aspect of ancient Greek social life. The *xenos*, or "guest-friend," usually from another Greek city-state, was both welcomed and protected by someone in the host city. In classical Greece, scholar Richard Buxton writes, long-range travelers most often lacked "all the social ties which made existence practical when they were at home." Alone in a strange town, they commonly had nowhere to turn for companionship and sometimes even for some of their most basic needs. Thus, "the institution of *xenia* (guest-friendship) was of enormous practical and emotional significance."[19]

WORD ORIGINS

xenos

In ancient Greece: a foreigner treated with hospitality.

In modern life: xenophobia, fear or distrust of foreigners.

This hospitality system had universally recognized rules. People were expected, even socially obligated, to take in foreigners or other strangers and offer them at least one meal, plus a bed for the night. Moreover, Buxton adds, these "obligations could be ignored only at great peril. In myths, those who break *xenia* invariably suffer for it."[20] Zeus's drowning of Baucis's and Philemon's neighbors was a classic example of heaven-sent punishment for ignoring the social duty to be hospitable. The tale also demonstrates how most Greeks believed natural disasters were not random events, but rather expressions of divine displeasure.

Chapter Two

The Celestial Sphere

One of the major goals of modern science, especially the discipline of astronomy, is to explain the workings of the universe, or cosmos, including the trillions of stars, galaxies, planets, and other objects within it. Similarly, the main object of a fair proportion of Greek myths was to make various objects and phenomena that ancient people observed in the heavens more understandable. To Greece's earliest inhabitants, the sky's vast curved surface, or celestial sphere, was both mysterious and awe inspiring. People were fascinated by the daily movements of the sun, moon, stars, and planets and quite naturally wondered what these objects were. They were also eager to know where the sun went at night and why the moon changed its shape over the course of each month.

The myths that offered answers to such questions developed long before the rise of the first scientists. Not surprisingly, therefore, those tales were based on primitive, mistaken assumptions about nature and celestial phenomena. Perhaps the most basic of these conjectures was that earthly lands, seas, and societies—that is, the known world—lay at the center of all things. Consequently, the celestial sphere must both enclose and exist for the benefit of the world's residents.

A second assumption about the heavens present in the Greek myths was that they were made of some solid, or at least "touchable," material. Often those stories described the sky as a huge dome composed of bronze, an alloy (mixture) of copper and tin. This made sense, since most of the Greek myths derived from the era directly following the collapse of Greece's Bronze Age civilization. Clearly, the objects on or near that sphere slowly moved across the sky from east to west each day.

The myths made it clear that those objects did not move of their own accord. Rather, somebody or something caused such movement, along with other events that occurred in the heavens. It was only a small logical leap from that idea to the notion that one or more gods were behind it all. Thus, there were multiple myths about the early Titan Atlas, a giant who supposedly held up the sky's western section while standing in what is now Morocco, in North Africa. Also, specific heavenly bodies were either manifestations, or varied forms, of gods or else controlled by them.

Helios's and Selene's Chariots

Of those heavenly entities, most conspicuous of all was the sun, represented by the god Helios, who appeared in numerous myths. These stories described him not only as the handsome sun god, but also as the protector of the oaths that humans swore and the inventor of the four-horse chariot. It was said he lived in a splendid palace situated along the far eastern shore of the Ocean, the river-like waterway that supposedly encircled Earth's land portions.

Each day at dawn Helios left his palace and drove his magnificent four-horse chariot across the sky. According to one myth, as he glanced down he could see and hear everything happening on Earth below. Eventually, he reached and slipped below the western horizon, climbed from his chariot, and entered a large golden cup. That gleaming chalice then whisked him around the northern shores of the Ocean and back to his palace in the east.

Another of Helios's well-known myths was the one in which his half-mortal son Phaethon talked him into allowing that young man to drive the four-horse chariot across the sky. Shortly after heading for the airy region near the inner surface of the great bronze sky-dome, Phaethon lost control of the vehicle. In a state of panic, the

> ## WORD ORIGINS
>
> ### panic
>
> In modern life: fear or dread; panicky.
>
> In ancient Greece: *panikos*, meaning extreme fear.

Phaethon drove Helios's chariot across the sky but lost control of the vehicle, causing the panicked horses to drag it downward and set part of Earth ablaze. Zeus intervened by throwing a thunderbolt at Phaethon, killing him but saving Earth.

four normally stalwart steeds dragged the careening cart in a wild ride that set some of Earth's surface ablaze.

The commotion soon caught the attention of the master of Mount Olympus, mighty Zeus. Feeling he had no choice but to intervene, he leapt off the towering peak and in a single bound reached a point a few miles below the soaring chariot. Reaching into his tunic, the god removed a sparkling thunderbolt and, aiming it like a javelin, hurled it upward. The missile struck Phaethon in the chest, frying him like a boar on a spit, and his charred body plummeted downward into a river. Seconds later, Helios, who was not as fast as Zeus, caught up to the chariot and managed to bring the rampaging stallions under control.

Helios's sister, Selene, goddess of the moon, soon learned about the harrowing incident. She also drove a chariot, but hers was drawn by two, rather than four, winged horses. Some Greek artists pictured her riding atop a single steed rather than in a chariot. In addition,

Myth-Tellers' Corner: Ovid

Ovid was the popular nickname for the great Roman poet and mythographer (myth-teller) Publius Ovidius Naso. Born in 43 BCE, he became widely popular for his humorous, often clever verses about love and sexual relations. Some of these writings were so frank and graphic that people of more traditional sensibilities criticized him. Unfortunately for Ovid, the then ruling first emperor, Augustus, was one of those critics. The ruler cautioned the writer several times to tone down his poems, but these warnings fell on deaf ears. So in 8 CE Ovid found himself banished to a bleak little town on the shores of the faraway Black Sea, where he spent the last nine years of his life.

In addition to his many love poems, Ovid turned out a collection of fresh tellings of old Greek myths. Titled the *Metamorphoses*, it was more comprehensive than any other ancient mythology anthology. "No ancient writer can compare with him in this respect," the late, acclaimed myth-teller Edith Hamilton wrote. "He told almost all the stories and he told them at great length. Occasionally stories familiar to us through literature and art have come down to us only in his pages." Ovid's fame and high esteem as a myth-teller extended beyond the end of the ancient world, and he was particularly beloved during the European Renaissance (circa 1350–1600). Then and later, his collection of myths powerfully influenced all manner of poets and playwrights, including England's equally immortal William Shakespeare.

Edith Hamilton, *Mythology.* New York: Grand Central, 2011, p. 21.

they frequently depicted her wearing a crown shaped like the moon's slender crescent phase.

Some of Selene's myths had little or nothing to do with the moon itself. For example, several ancient authors recounted her love affair with a young, handsome Greek shepherd named Endymion, with whom she was said to have had fifty children. Another myth claimed that she raised the monstrous Nemean Lion in a cave and was upset when the heroic strongman Heracles slew the beast. Selene's greatest claim to fame, however, remained her association with the moon's silver-white orb. A surviving hymn to her captures the degree to which the Greeks viewed her as the visually stunning embodiment of that dominant object of the night sky:

> From her immortal head a radiance is shown from heaven and embraces earth. And great is the beauty that arises from her shining light. The air, unlit before, glows with the light of her golden crown, and her rays beam clear, whenever bright Selene, having bathed her lovely body in the waters of Ocean, and donned her far-gleaming raiment, and yoked her strong-necked, shining team, and drives on her long-maned horses at full speed, in the evening in the mid-month. Then her great orbit is full and then her beams shine brightest as she increases. So she is a sure token and a sign to mortal men.[21]

The Early Cosmic View

For the classical Greeks, the myths about Helios, Selene, and other gods and goddesses associated with the heavenly bodies did more than show what those objects were and how they moved. Those ancient tales also clarified how certain phenomena that people observed around them came to be. In a way, therefore, some myths were the classical Greek equivalent of modern science texts dealing with natural phenomena.

For instance, the myth of young Phaethon's wild ride on Helios's chariot explained why Africans who lived south of Egypt and the Sahara Desert had dark skin. Supposedly, their ancestors' skins had been scorched black by the heat generated by the careening chariot as it grazed Earth's surface. Phaethon's myth also provided an explanation for the origin of the Milky Way. That elongated, hazy, faint patch of light visible in the sky on a clear night is now known to be the combined glow of millions of stars too faint to be seen singly by the naked eye. To the classical Greeks, however, the Milky Way was the still glowing scar that Phaethon's chariot had etched into the sky-dome's bronze surface.

Other myths that mentioned natural phenomena also contributed to the early classical Greeks' cosmic view, or overall vision of the cosmos. They developed it well before the rise of Greek science in the 500s, 400s, and 300s BCE. That early, prescientific vision included an elaborate cosmology, or general conception of the universe's structure. Initially, like many other ancient peoples, the Greeks visualized Earth as a huge, flat, circular landform. On its surface rested forests, lakes, mountains, animals, cities, and humans.

Above that landform loomed the sky-dome and the sun, moon, stars, and other heavenly bodies. The early classical Greeks believed that after the heavenly objects traversed the sky and dipped below the horizon, they traveled beneath Earth's surface and skirted the underworld. Then, at some point, they passed through the subterranean portion of the Ocean, which on the surface encircled the known world. Those underground waters supposedly purified the celestial objects, preparing them to rise back up into the sky in the next leg of their endlessly recurring daily cycle.

The Stars and Divine Fire

In addition to the sun and moon, identified with Helios and Selene respectively, the Greeks recognized large numbers of tiny points of light in the night sky. They called each an *aster*, a term that eventually morphed into the English word *star*. A number of myths mentioned the origins and identities of the stars. Among those tales were a few cited by the seventh-century-BCE epic poet Hesiod and others summarized later by the third-century-BCE Greek poet Aratus of Soli.

According to Aratus, Zeus originally set the stars in the sky in separate groups, called both constellations and signs. It was he, Aratus said, "who set the signs in heaven, and marked out the constellations, and for the year devised what stars chiefly should give to men right signs of the seasons." People should give thanks to Zeus for doing that, Aratus stated, and he went on to praise the god, saying, "Hail, O Father, mighty marvel, mighty blessing unto men. Hail to you and to the elder race," that is, the gods themselves. Because of the efforts of those superior beings, the poet added, the stars "are drawn across the heavens always, through all time continually!"[22]

As for what the stars *were*, the early classical Greeks envisioned them as hollow wheels, or holes in the sky's inner surface. The wheels were thought to contain fire. It was not ordinary fire, however, but rather so-called divine fire, an extremely hot and bright variety that the gods themselves manufactured. One view was that the heavenly fire resided inside the wheels; another claimed it existed behind the stars, in the portion of the heavens lying outside the sky-dome. In either case, a little bit of brightness showed through each of the thousands of tiny holes in

Pictured are the planets of our solar system. The early Greeks were aware that five special stars moved slowly through the sky, from one constellation to another; people sometimes called the planets wandering stars.

Cetus the Sea Monster

The constellation Cetus is sometimes identified as a whale. But in the original Greek myth that inspired it, the creature is a sea monster sent by Poseidon, lord of the oceans, to punish the land of Ethiopia, in northeastern Africa. The local queen, Cassiopeia, had bragged that her daughter Andromeda was more beautiful than some female sea gods. Hoping to prevent Poseidon from destroying the entire country, Ethiopian officials chained Andromeda to a rock. There she awaited the arrival of the bloodthirsty Cetus, which Poseidon sent to devour her. However, at that moment the hero Perseus was returning from slaying the monster Medusa. That female creature had been so hideous that merely gazing at her had caused people or animals to turn to stone. One version of Andromeda's myth claims that Perseus held up Medusa's head to Cetus, which swiftly turned the sea monster to stone. In another version, the hero, flying by means of winged sandals, used his sword to dispatch the marine monster. According to Ovid:

> Swooping swiftly through the sky, Perseus attacked the monster's back and, to the sound of its bellowing, buried his sword up to its crooked hilt in the beast's right shoulder. Tormented by this deep wound, the creature now reared itself upright, high in the air, and plunged beneath the waters. [But] the hero, on his swift wings, [pursued it and] dealt blows with his curved sword. [In all], four times he drove the weapon through the beast's flanks, striking it again and again.

Ovid, *Metamorphoses,* trans. Mary M. Innes. New York: Penguin, 2006, p. 113.

the sky. Some holes were slightly bigger than others, the common wisdom held, which explained why some stars were brighter than others.

All of the world's primitive ancient peoples, including the early Greeks, were aware that five special stars existed among the many ordinary ones. Today known as the planets, they moved slowly through the sky, from one constellation to another. So people sometimes called the planets wandering stars. "Of quite a different class are those five other orbs," Aratus wrote, which "pursue a shifty course, and long are the periods of their revolution"[23] through the constellations.

Each planet was identified with and thought to be controlled by a certain god. They were Hermes (now known by its Roman name, Mercury); Aphrodite (Venus); Ares (Mars); Zeus (Jupiter); and Cronos (Saturn). Of the other three planets recognized today, the Greeks did not know about Uranus and Neptune because they were too faint to see with the naked eye, and they did not realize that Earth is a planet.

The Constellations and Astrology

The Greeks pictured the constellations through which the planets moved mostly as images of noted mythical characters and animals, and those same identifications are still widely recognized today. The Greeks did not invent them all, however. Rather, they borrowed many from the older civilizations of western Asia, including those of the Sumerians and Assyrians, in what is now Iraq. Nevertheless, the early Greeks did have their own myths describing the origins of specific constellations.

Also, the Greeks viewed those star groups as more than mere outlines made up of tiny bright dots. Rather, even well into the classical period, they saw those distinctive images as living, spirit-like beings. It was thought that, having been endowed with immortality by Zeus or another god, each constellation was conscious and aware that it inhabited the heavens.

In addition, each constellation was associated with at least one myth and in some cases several. One of the better-known examples—Capricorn—originated in a myth that described it as a minor sea deity resembling a goat. It hurried to Zeus's aid when that leader of the Olympian gods engaged in battle with the first race of deities—the Titans.

The ancient Greeks believed the twelve constellations of the zodiac (pictured) had a direct effect on the lives of human beings. This was a fundamental principle behind astrology, which was extremely popular among the classical Greeks.

During that calamitous conflict, Capricorn's odd body—which mixed the traits of goats and fish—scared several of the Titans, weakening their ranks. According to the second-century-CE Roman myth-teller now known as Pseudo-Hyginus, "When Zeus attacked the Titans, Capricorn is said to have cast into the enemy the fear that is called panic." Not only did the little being's physical form upset the Titans, the goat-fish also "hurled shellfish against the enemy,"[24] a novel approach to warfare. To thank it for this help, Zeus set Capricorn in the sky as one of the constellations of the zodiac.

The twelve constellations of the zodiac, which the Greeks called the *zodiakos*, form a broad, circular band running around the celestial sphere. Those star groups are roughly centered on the ecliptic, the apparent path the sun takes as it slowly changes its position relative to the stars during the course of a year. Ancient peoples, the Greeks among them, came to associate those twelve myth-based star groups with predicting people's fates. It was thought that a constellation's supposed living attributes and connection to the divine had a direct effect on the lives of human beings. These were the fundamental principles behind the pseudoscience of astrology, which over time became extremely popular among the classical and later ancient Greeks.

A Charming Myth-Based Vision

Another well-known zodiacal constellation based on myths widely familiar to all Greeks was Gemini, the twins. That term referred to the fact that two of Zeus's sons—Castor and Polydeuces, together called the Dioscuri—were twin brothers. In one myth, the two were skilled horsemen who sailed with the renowned hero Jason to find the Golden Fleece, the hide of a magical ram. In another ancient tale, they helped sailors at sea during storms by taking the form of Saint Elmo's fire. A kind of electrical energy, it is sometimes seen glowing eerily along ships' masts and rigging during storms. An ancient hymn dedicated to the Dioscuri states in part that the two brothers "are seen darting through the air on tawny wings [as Saint Elmo's fire]. They [immediately] allay the blasts of the cruel winds and still the waves upon the surface of the white sea. Fair signs are they and deliverance from toil. And when the shipmen see them they are glad and have rest from their pain and labor."[25] Following the twins' death, Zeus transferred them into the sky, where their still-living souls formed the constellation Gemini.

As in the cases of many other ancient constellations, Zeus placed Castor and Polydeuces in the sky to commemorate their good deeds or other feats as told in their myths. Particularly prominent were the star groups connected with the famous, muscular hero Heracles, whom the Romans later called Hercules. After he defeated and killed the fierce Nemean Lion, it became the zodiacal constellation Leo (Latin for "lion"). Similarly, when Heracles slew the Hydra, a dragon with nine heads, it became the constellation that still bears the name Hydra today. Interestingly, in the myth in which the hero and dragon fought, an ornery crab bit the man's foot, prompting him to step on and crush the crusty crustacean. Zeus's wife, Hera, who hated Heracles, then put the crab in the sky as the constellation Cancer, to honor the creature for at least *trying* to defeat the strongman.

In contrast, sometimes an earthly character ended up as a constellation as a sort of afterthought, when his or her myth grew directly out of that of another, better-known figure. A well-known example is the star group Cygnus, the swan. The classical Greeks associated that constellation with the tale of Phaethon's riotous ride across the sky and plunge to his death in a river. In a separate myth that grew from Phaethon's story, his brother Cygnus (or Cycnus) was naturally grief-stricken over what had happened. For days following his sibling's death, loving and faithful Cygnus dove down into the river and collected the deceased's body parts. Finding them allowed Cygnus and his relatives to hold a proper funeral for Phaethon. The gods took note of Cygnus's decency and devotion to his brother and rewarded him in an unexpected way. According to the first-century-BCE Roman myth-teller Ovid, as Cygnus mourned, "his voice became thin and shrill, and white feathers hid his hair. His neck grew long, stretching out from his breast, his fingers reddened, and a membrane joined them together. Wings clothed his sides, and a blunt beak fastened on his mouth. Cygnus became a new kind of bird."[26] Not long afterward, Cygnus found himself in the sky as a graceful swan soaring above the known world. There, he took his place alongside the sun, moon, planets, and other star groups in the classical Greeks' neat and charming myth-based vision of the vast and timeless celestial sphere.

Chapter Three

⌐⌐⌐⌐⌐⌐⌐⌐⌐⌐⌐⌐⌐⌐⌐⌐⌐⌐⌐⌐⌐⌐⌐⌐⌐⌐⌐⌐⌐⌐⌐⌐⌐

Fire and the Seasons

Among the most important natural phenomena recognized and utilized by the ancient Greeks were fire and the changing seasons. They employed fire in a number of ways, among them to cook their food, create tools and weapons, and burn the bodies of animals in religious sacrifices. Meanwhile, they learned to exploit the changing seasons in the growing of life-giving crops.

As in the cases of other kinds of natural forces and phenomena, the existence of both fire and the seasons was explained in myths that all Greeks learned in their childhood. According to one famous tale, humanity owed its ability to use fire to an early god named Prometheus. Divine beings—namely the agricultural goddess Demeter and her daughter, Persephone—were also responsible for giving rise to the seasons. These two stories were among the longest, most detailed, and crucial of all the ancient Greek myths. It is not surprising, therefore, that they influenced numerous classical Greek customs and practices.

Prometheus the Creator

The protagonist, or leading character, in the first of these two crucial myths, Prometheus, was one of the Titans, the first race of gods the ancient Greeks recognized. Long before humans appeared on the scene, there was a great battle between the Titans and the Olympian

⌐⌐⌐⌐⌐⌐⌐⌐⌐⌐⌐⌐⌐⌐⌐⌐⌐⌐⌐⌐⌐⌐⌐⌐⌐⌐⌐⌐⌐⌐

gods led by Zeus. In that conflict, which the classical Greeks called the Titanomachy, Prometheus took Zeus's side. After the Olympians won and consigned their enemies to the underworld's deepest layer, Zeus came to appreciate Prometheus for another reason as well.

Namely, the young Titan had a great deal of *sophia*, or wisdom, in part because he could perceive certain future trends and events. Indeed, his very name meant "forethought," or "seeing what is to come." That prompted Zeus to make Prometheus his chief adviser.

Numerous ancient accounts say that eventually Zeus asked his advisor to create a race of mortal men and women, and Prometheus fashioned their bodies from mud or clay (*argillos*). Then Zeus's daughter Athena and some other gods contributed the breath of life and other qualities that shaped the new creatures. One problem was that the initial humans lacked the strength, speed, warm fur, keen sense of smell, and other useful qualities that allowed most animals to survive in a harsh environment. The result was that the "creatures of Prometheus," as Zeus called the humans, were often hungry, cold, and miserable. As Prometheus himself put it (in Aeschylus's play *Prometheus Bound*), "All their length of life they passed like shapes in dreams, confused and purposeless. Of brick-built, sun-warmed houses, or of carpentry, they had no notion. [Instead, they] lived in holes, like swarms of ants, or deep in sunless caverns. [They] knew no way to mark off winter, or flowery spring, or fruitful summer. Their every act was without knowledge."[27]

This state of affairs saddened Prometheus, who came to care a great deal for his new creations. He realized that if the humans had fire, they would be able to make weapons with which to hunt and tools with which to make shelters and fashion a civilization. So he asked Zeus for permission to introduce fire to the human race. But the leader of the gods forbade this. Zeus insisted that fire must always belong only to the immortal and superior gods.

WORD ORIGINS

sophia

In ancient Greece: wisdom, or knowledge.

In modern life: philosophy, the study of the nature of existence and knowledge.

An Awful Punishment

Prometheus initially tried to obey Zeus. But as time went on, the Titan kept returning to the soft spot he held in his heart for the nearly helpless two-legged creatures he had fashioned from mud. So one day Prometheus stealthily went to one of the forges the gods operated on Mount Olympus. Hiding some embers from the divine fire in a hollow plant stalk, he made his way to Earth's surface, where he showed some of the humans how to start a fire. Prometheus also instructed them in how to construct hearths and forges and make weapons and tools.

Myth-Tellers' Corner: Aeschylus

Born in Athens in about 525 BCE, Aeschylus is widely acknowledged to have been the world's first important and influential playwright. Together with the younger Sophocles and Euripides, he was one of the three great writers of tragedy during Athens's cultural outburst of the fifth century BCE. In 490 BCE, Aeschylus fought in the pivotal battle of Marathon, where the Athenians defeated a Persian invasion force. Ten years later, when he was about fifty, he was also in the military ranks during the naval engagement at Salamis (near Athens), in which the Greeks demolished the Persian navy. He described that crucial event in riveting detail a few years later in his play *The Persians*.

That work is one of only seven of Aeschylus's surviving plays, out of eighty or more. The others are *Agamemnon* (458 BCE), *The Libation Bearers* (458 BCE), *The Eumenides* (458 BCE), *Seven Against Thebes* (467 BCE), *The Suppliant Women* (circa 463 BCE), and *Prometheus Bound* (circa 460 BCE). The traditional Greek myths provided the background stories for all of these splendid dramas. In addition to writing, Aeschylus developed several theatrical concepts, including the "second actor." Prior to him, a single actor played all of the characters by donning different masks. Using a second actor, who also wore diverse masks, allowed a playwright to show more characters and thereby tell a story in more depth.

At first, Zeus and most other deities paid little attention to the humans, so they did not know the mortals were employing fire and building a civilization. But eventually Zeus did find out. Very upset, he questioned Prometheus, who freely admitted what he had done. Aeschylus had the Titan say, "I am he who hunted out the source of fire, and stole it, packed in the pith of a dry fennel-stalk. And fire has proved for men a teacher of every art, their grand resource."[28]

Zeus was so angry that he inflicted an awful punishment on Prometheus. The chief Olympian ordered two giants, named Force and

Prometheus, chief advisor to Zeus, gave humans fire against Zeus's orders and taught them to build forges and make weapons and tools. In response, an angry Zeus had Prometheus chained to a rock, where a vulture devoured his liver each day.

Violence, to arrest the Titan and transport him to a remote, mountainous area lying northeast of the Greek-speaking lands. Also at Zeus's command, Hephaestos, god of the forge, chained Prometheus to a large, flat rock. There, early each morning an ugly, hungry vulture (in some ancient sources an eagle) appeared and chewed out his liver. That night the organ grew back. But the next morning the huge bird returned and consumed the god's liver once more, causing him gnawing pain day after day, month after month, year after year.

More than once, the lord of Olympus offered to end this horrendous torture. All the chained god had to do was admit he was wrong and submit completely to Zeus's will. Brave Prometheus refused to give in, however, and made it clear that he would rather suffer that way for eternity than give in to tyranny and injustice. Fortunately for him, he did not have to endure Zeus's pun-

> ## WORD ORIGINS
>
> ### *argillos*
>
> In ancient Greece: clay.
>
> In modern life: argillite, a fine-grained kind of rock made up of compressed clay particles.

ishment forever. A few months later the bighearted strongman Heracles happened by and freed the Titan from his servitude on the rock. (In the spellbinding climax of Aeschylus's play, the mountaintop, with Prometheus still chained to it, collapses and disappears into the depths.)

Making Civilization Possible

When the Athenians and other classical Greeks watched this incredible drama unfold onstage, they were both moved and inspired by Prometheus's courage in the face of cruelty and injustice. They felt much sympathy and gratitude for the Titan's sacrifice for the humans he had created. Yet the Greeks' appreciation for Prometheus's gift of fire went well beyond mere sympathy for his loyalty and suffering for the human race. That gift, they firmly believed, had made their very civilization possible. Indeed, fire was essential to metalworking, which produced weapons for hunting and defense, as well as a wide array of tools for food preparation and consumption, constructing buildings, and producing all manner of crafts.

Fire was also integral to classical Greek religion. The central ritual of that faith was sacrifice, or making offerings to one or more gods to either ensure those deities' support or pacify their wrath. A number of different kinds of things could be sacrificed in these rituals. By far the most common approach was to offer the gods animals—most often sheep, goats, cattle, rabbits, and birds. Fire was used in each successive stage of the ritual, as can be seen in the following description of a typical Greek animal sacrifice by noted archaeologist Lesley Adkins (the "victim" to which she refers was the animal being offered):

> Unground barleycorn was sprinkled over the victim, altar, and possibly the participants. Hair was cut from the victim's head and burned on the altar. The victim was then killed with a blow from an ax, and its throat was cut. Blood was collected in a bowl and splashed on the altar. The animal was then butchered and the portion selected for the god was burned on the altar . . . while wine was simultaneously poured into the flames. The entrails [organs] were cooked separately and tasted first, then the remaining meat was cooked and eaten by the participants in a sacrificial feast at which the god was regarded as an honored guest.[29]

A Daughter's Frantic Cry

Among the many existing natural phenomena, no less important than fire in maintaining classical Greek civilization was the passage of the *horae*, or seasons, which made growing crops practical. Just as Prometheus's myth explained how humans came to exploit fire, an equally crucial tale cited the origins of the seasons. Central to that tale was Demeter, goddess of plants, and particularly grains, which were a staple of the ancient Greek diet. Because she made these and other crops possible, the Greeks viewed her as a giver of the gifts of life.

Demeter's principal story was one of the most famous, beloved, and enduring of all the Greek myths. It began with a secret, highly unfair, and thoughtless bargain struck between Zeus and his brother,

---

WORD ORIGINS

horae

In ancient Greece: the seasons.

In modern life: horoscope, a diagram based on the positions of the sun, moon, and constellations during the different months and seasons.

Lord of the underworld Hades desired Persephone, Demeter's young daughter, as his bride. So he abducted her while she was walking in a meadow and took her back to the underworld in his golden chariot.

Hades, lord of the underworld. Hades expressed his desire to have Demeter's young daughter, Persephone, as his wife, and Zeus gave his permission.

As a result, when Persephone was out walking in a pleasant meadow one day, the earth suddenly cracked open and Hades appeared atop his golden chariot. Snatching the surprised young woman, the god directed his fierce black horses to carry them deep underground. Just before they disappeared beneath the earth, Persephone called out, and her divine mother, situated many miles distant, heard

Sympathy for Prometheus's Plight

The classical Greeks not only identified with their creator, the Titan Prometheus, but also sympathized with his plight when Zeus punished him for giving the secret of fire to early humans. The evidence for this is abundant in surviving examples of classical Greek literature. Yet perhaps no other writing from that period reflects how most Greeks felt about Prometheus's predicament more than Aeschylus's magnificent play *Prometheus Bound*. The entire work is in a general sense a paean, or hymn, to the Titan's heroism and courage. But in certain key speeches, Aeschylus more specifically speaks for all Greeks in pointing out Zeus's unfairness.

The following lines are delivered by the members of the chorus. Greek playwrights often employed them as supposedly unbiased observers who stood on onstage and both observed and commented (in unison) on the characters' actions. At one point the chorus members address Prometheus, saying, "Sudden fear fills my eyes to see your body withering on this rock." Zeus had once been just in all things, they remark. But "these are new laws indeed by which Zeus tyrannically rules." Moreover, "only a heart of iron, a temper carved from rock, Prometheus, could refuse compassion for your pains. Had I known, I could have wished never to see this sight. Now that I have seen it, sorrow and anger wrack my heart."

Aeschylus, *Prometheus Bound*, in *Aeschylus: Prometheus Bound, the Suppliants, Seven Against Thebes, the Persians*, trans. Philip Vellacott. Baltimore: Penguin, 1961, pp. 25, 27.

that frantic cry. "Bitter pain seized her heart," according to one ancient account. Leaping into the air, she "sped like a wild bird over the firm land and yielding sea, seeking her child. But no one would tell her the truth, neither god nor mortal man." No one "came with true news for her."[30]

After several days, however, Demeter sought out Helios, the handsome sun god. She reasoned that he must have witnessed what had happened from his vantage high above the earth's surface. Sure enough, he told her that Hades had abducted her daughter and carried her away into the dark underworld.

A Fateful Deal

Furious and sick with worry, Demeter lashed out in her grief. No longer did she ensure that fresh fields of grain would grow, but instead allowed terrible droughts to sweep across all lands. As many people began to starve, Zeus and other gods attempted to calm her. But she would hear none of it. Shunning Mount Olympus, she assumed the form of an old woman and wandered from one city to another for what seemed to her like endless months.

Eventually, Demeter stopped to rest for a while in Eleusis, a small town lying not far west of Athens. The residents were kind to her, so she decided to stay indefinitely. Revealing her true identity, she asked them to erect a temple where she could live, and when it was completed she locked herself inside and brooded unhappily for many months.

Outside, meanwhile, the world's surface grew barren and no more grain or other crops would grow. Desperate, various gods again tried to convince Demeter to give in and allow fertility to return, or else, they said, humanity might perish. But as the same ancient account relates, "She stubbornly rejected all their words, for she vowed that she would never set foot on fragrant Olympus nor let fruit [grow] out of the ground, until she beheld with her eyes her own fair-faced daughter."[31]

Finally, Zeus and Hades realized that they must find some way to appease Demeter. Otherwise, the human race would die out, and the immortal deities would lose the pleasant benefit of being worshipped on a regular basis. Zeus oversaw a fateful deal struck between Hades and Demeter. It held that Persephone would divide her residence equally between the earth's sunlit surface and the dark reaches of Hades's subterranean kingdom. When she lived with her mother on the surface, it would be spring and summer, and warm winds would blow and crops would grow. But when she dwelled with her new husband, fall and winter would bring cold and desolation to the world and the land would be barren.

Demeter's "Good Gifts"

In this way, the classical Greeks believed, Demeter earned her frequently quoted epithet (nickname) of "giver of good gifts, and bringer of the seasons."[32] These items were inescapably linked. After all, the "gifts" of the crops the Greeks grew and consumed depended on farmers' exploitation of the passage of the seasons. Greek farmers took advantage of a natural cycle involving water, soil nutrients, and sunshine connected directly to seasonal change. For example, they learned to plant barley and wheat in October during the long fall season that preceded the oncoming winter. To prepare the ground, they used wooden plows with iron blades. Guided by an experienced planter, oxen or mules pulled the plows, while one or two assistants followed, flinging the seeds into the newly dug furrows as they walked.

Those seeds rested in the rich soil for the rest of the fall and into winter, which happens to be Greece's primary rainy season. Safe beneath the surface during that shortest of the seasons, the seeds had the nutrients and water they needed to germinate and thrive. The grains broke the surface in March and were harvested in April or May, during the longish spring season. After cutting down the grain, farmworkers gathered it into bundles and took it to a barn for threshing (separating the edible part from the husks and stalks). This process was accomplished by having mules trample the grain on a stone floor.

The other principal crops in Greece were olives and grapes. Farmers harvested olives from trees between October and January both by knocking them down with sticks and picking them by hand. In contrast, people harvested grapes, which grew on vines, in September, near the end of the warm summer season. Workers crushed the grapes by foot, a process that remains in use today in Greece and other Mediterranean lands.

The Power of Myths

Demeter's main myth was also the basis for a religious tradition featuring ceremonies that took place on Athenian soil but attracted Greeks from numerous other city-states. Known as the "Eleusinian Myster-

Olives were one of the principal crops in classical Greece; farmers harvested olives from trees between October and January, picking them by hand or knocking them from the trees with sticks.

ies," it was centered in the town of Eleusis, which in the myth was where the goddess settled after leaving Mount Olympus. Followers of the Mysteries met in her temple there, which the locals expanded and maintained all through classical times and well beyond.

With the aid of a priesthood, each September the Eleusinian cult, or congregation, held a sacred festival celebrating Demeter's loss of and eventual reunion with her daughter Persephone. New members, or trainees, underwent a top secret initiation (one still unknown today), which explains why people called the sect the "Mysteries." Anyone could join—male, female, free, or slave.

After their initiation, the trainees bathed in the sea, which supposedly purified them of prior sins. Then they sacrificed a pig to the goddess. Later, they and the rest of the members marched in a stately procession from Athens to Demeter's temple in Eleusis, a distance of some 12 miles (19 km). As they walked, they carried various sacred objects, the identity of which remains unclear to this day. The climax of the celebration appears to have consisted of a priest showing the sacred objects to the members. This specialized worship of Demeter, based directly on her chief myth, remained popular among generations of Greeks until nearly the close of the ancient era. Its long history demonstrates the extraordinary power of myths from the dim past over Greek life during and well after the classical era.

Chapter Four

Plants and Animals

In his famous, massive collection of Greek myths—the *Metamorphoses*—the great Roman poet and storyteller Ovid sought to recount tales of humans who underwent various transformations. He particularly reveled in stories of people who for one reason or another ended up as *zoia* (animals) or as plants. Other ancient writers told some of these same stories, so frequently two or more versions of those myths survived into later ages. One of the more famous of these storytellers was a man named Aesop, about whose life nothing is known for certain. His charming animal tales, each with a simple moral, are still read with delight by people worldwide.

A major point that Ovid, Aesop, and other ancient myth-tellers made was that a fair number of plants and animals did not come into the world in the forms known to the classical Greeks. Rather, long before, in the Age of Heroes or even before that, they had taken other forms. The manner in which they transformed into new shapes and varieties was widely thought to be explained in traditional myths.

> ## WORD ORIGINS
>
> ### ZOO
>
> In modern life: a place where people go to see animals on exhibit.
>
> In ancient Greece: *zoia*, meaning animals.

The Hyacinth and Lost Friendship

For instance, it was said that the hyacinth plant originated from the transformation of a boy named Hyacinthus into a plant. The young man hailed from the famous militaristic city-state of Sparta, in southern Greece. Apollo, god of prophecy, the story went, befriended Hyacinthus and one day challenged him to a contest in throwing the discus. Apollo threw first. According to Ovid, he "flung it through the air. Its weight scattered the clouds in its path and then, after a long time, it fell back again" to the ground. "Immediately, the young Spartan, in

According to Greek myths, the hyacinth plant came to be after the god Apollo accidentally killed a boy named Hyacinthus in a discus-throwing contest. The mourning Apollo transformed the boy into a plant with markings that symbolized his grief.

his eagerness for the game, ran forward without stopping to think, in a hurry to pick up the discus. But it bounced back off the hard ground, and rose into the air, striking him full in the face. The god grew as pale as the boy himself."[33]

Apollo rushed to the boy's side and tried to stop the bleeding. But it was no use. "The wound was beyond any cure," Ovid went on, and the boy slipped away into the realm of death. The mourning god cried out, "I wish that I might give my life in exchange for yours, as you so well deserve, or die along with you! But since I am bound by the laws of fate, that cannot be. Still, you will always be with me, your name constantly upon my lips, never forgotten." In a dramatic voice, Apollo declared, "You will be changed into a new kind of flower and will show markings that imitate my sobs. Further, a time will come when the bravest of heroes will be connected with this flower."[34]

That beautiful plant "took on the shape of a lily," Ovid added. "But it was purple in color, whereas lilies are silvery white."[35] Moreover, true to his promise, Apollo made the flower's markings mimic his grief-stricken cries. The "ai ai" markings on the hyacinth, said to imitate Apollo's sobs, ever after stood for "alas, alas."

The classical Greeks, who frequently displayed a sentimental streak, enjoyed repeating this old tale, in part because it was about strong bonds of friendship and the sad loss of a loved one. Over time, storytellers altered the theme a bit. Thus, although the story was originally about the companionship between the god and the boy, society came to associate the hyacinth with the feelings of desire between a young bride and groom. Indeed, people sometimes joked about the flower's effectiveness as a love potion. There was even an old saying that suggested it was not very potent. A simple hyacinth bulb, it went, could not help a young man who was not already eager to be with his bride.

Such beliefs about the hyacinth persisted, in somewhat modified form, into the centuries immediately following the classical era, when Rome conquered the Greek lands. In Roman times it became common for Greeks and Romans in a wedding party to prepare a dish made from hyacinth bulbs for young newlyweds. Supposedly, it would make them more enthusiastic to make love and have children for the good of society.

The Origin of the Daffodil

The classical Greeks learned about the genesis of another well-known *anthos*, or flower—the daffodil—in the famous myth of Narcissus. He was the son of the nymph Liriope. Nymphs, minor nature goddesses who numbered in the thousands, were divided into groups corresponding to various natural phenomena. Liriope belonged to the Naiads, who were thought to inhabit streams, wells, fountains, and other freshwater sources.

All of the nymphs were highly attractive. So it is not surprising that Liriope's son was himself extremely handsome. Indeed, Narcissus was so good-looking that many young nymphs, and human girls as well, fell in love with him. The problem was that he was extremely vain—so full of himself that he usually talked only about his own needs and tended to ignore his female companions.

Eventually, a nymph named Echo fell for Narcissus. Unfortunately for her, she had her own problem—namely that Hera, queen of the gods, had earlier removed her ability to speak normally. All she was able to do was repeat the last syllables of any words she heard. Hence, that natural phenomenon came to be called an *echo*, after her. As he had with other women, Narcissus paid little or no attention to Echo. Extremely hurt by his callous treatment of her, she refused to eat anything and as a result wasted away until only her voice—her echo—was left.

What neither Echo nor Narcissus had known was that the love goddess Aphrodite had been watching their relationship. That deity was so angry at Narcissus for his cruelty to Echo that she made him

WORD ORIGINS

narcissist

In modern life: a person who is overly impressed by him- or herself.

In ancient Greece: Narcissus, a mythical young man who was so in love with himself that he incessantly stared at his own reflection.

As punishment for his callous treatment of a nymph named Echo, the love goddess Aphrodite made Narcissus fall in love with his own reflection in a pool of water, where he knelt without interruption until he wasted away and died, giving rise to the first narcissus plant.

fall in love with his own reflection in a pool of water. Thereafter, without interruption, he knelt next to the pool and stared intently at himself. Because he did not eat, he wasted away and died, just as Echo had. Soon after his passing, the first narcissus plant, or daffodil flower, appeared on the spot where he had knelt. Also, over time people came to call someone who is very conceited a narcissist.

A Suitable Prize

A separate myth involving a nymph explained the source of another plant popular among the classical Greeks—the laurel. The nymph in question was beautiful Daphne, with whom Apollo, the handsome and stalwart god of prophecy, music, and poetry, fell madly in love.

Myth-Tellers' Corner: Aesop

Aesop's name has become synonymous with numerous charming ancient fables, usually about animals and often containing a simple but thoughtful moral. If he *was* a real person, which some modern experts still debate, it is notoriously difficult to pin down any concrete facts about his life. That includes his exact birth and death dates, which according to Greek tradition were sometime in the late 600s or early 500s BCE. Nevertheless, a few legends about Aesop survive. One claims he began life as a slave in Thrace, in extreme northern Greece. Eventually, according to that tale, he managed to gain his freedom and travel across the ancient world. Another ancient account holds that when he reached Lydia, in central Anatolia (what is now Turkey), the local ruler recognized his storytelling prowess and hired him as an entertainer in the Lydian royal court.

It remains unclear how many of Aesop's tales were based on ancient Greek or western Asian myths and how many he may have invented himself. Some of the more famous ones include "The Fox and the Grapes," "The Ants and the Grasshopper," "The Cat and the Mice," "The Ass and the Wolf," and "The Scorpion and the Frog." Probably the best known of his stories today is "The Hare and the Tortoise," which deals with a race between the title characters. The tortoise wins, and the moral, as nearly everyone knows, is that coolness and determination will prevail over haste and recklessness in the end.

To his regret, however, she had no interest in him. So each time he pursued her, she ran away.

One day, as Daphne was fleeing Apollo, she called on her father, a river god named Peneus, for help. Peneus promptly turned his daughter into a laurel tree in hopes that would cause Apollo to lose interest in her. In a sense it worked, because Apollo no longer chased her. However, his love for her did not dim, and in her memory he ordained that a laurel wreath would be used to crown the victors in athletic, musical, and poetry contests.

This myth was of great interest to the classical Greeks because they were in love with the idea of play and invented innumerable games to exploit that concept. The late, great scholar Edith Hamilton explained, "The Greeks were the first people in the world to play, and they played on a great scale. All over Greece there were games, all sorts of games: athletic contests of every description; races—horse-, boat-, foot-, torch-races; contests in music, where one side out-sung the other . . . games so many one grows weary with the list of them."[36]

Early on, the classical Greeks recognized that the winners of these competitions needed to be rewarded. Moreover, it should be in a manner that honored Apollo, who had instituted Greece's first athletic games at Delphi, site of his famous temple. So they reached into their myths and singled out what he had deemed a suitable prize for all contests—a simple laurel wreath.

Such wreaths were awarded to the winners of the events in the first Olympic Games, which tradition said occurred in 776 BCE at Olympia, in southwestern Greece. Similarly, all of the major Greek athletic games held in the centuries that followed employed laurel wreaths, a custom the Romans eventually adopted to award military victors. Julius Caesar (100–44 BCE) was perhaps the most renowned of the Roman military generals honored that way.

Origins of Water Creatures

The Greek myths explained the origins not only of various flowers and other plants, but also of several common animals. Some of the more interesting tales in that category involved creatures associated with water. The lowly frog, for instance, supposedly resulted from a mistake made by some ignorant country boys.

The story's main character was the minor goddess Leto, known best as the mother of the twin gods Apollo and Artemis—the result of an affair with Zeus. When the latter's wife, Hera, heard about the pregnancy, she angrily chased poor Leto from one earthly region to another. At one point, the mother-to-be stopped to rest beside a pond, and some local ruffians, unaware she was divine, bullied her. Irritated, Leto decided to teach them a lesson. According to Ovid, she waved her hand, and their throats suddenly grew "puffed and swollen" and their voices became "ill-natured croaks." Then their heads "shrank down onto their shoulders." Their "backs turned green and their bellies, the largest part of their bodies, were white. So they were changed into frogs, and, in their new shape, leaped about in the muddy pool."[37]

Another water creature, the dolphin, came about when Dionysus, deity of fertility and wine, was traveling through the Aegean Sea and asked some pirates to take him to the Greek island of Naxos. He assumed they would not be foolish enough to give a powerful god any trouble. But the pirates were unaware of his identity and thought he was a rich man they could hold for ransom. The brigands paid dearly for that mistake when he turned himself into a raging lion and chased them off the ship. Once they were in the sea, the still angry god turned them into dolphins.

That dolphins had descended from human pirates did not make the classical Greeks think badly of those magnificent sea creatures. In fact, Greek sailors, along with the many Greeks who dwelled on islands, admired and welcomed the appearance of dolphins. This was because those unusually intelligent marine mammals were widely viewed as signs of impending good fortune.

One reason for that widespread belief was an account by Herodotus about Arion, an early classical Greek poet who flourished sometime in the late 600s BCE. When Arion was on a ship far out at sea during a long trip, the account goes, some dishonest sailors took all his money. They then told him either to kill himself or jump overboard. Arion certainly did not want to end up in the water so far from land. As one noted historian writes, "No Greek would swim out into the deep from a boat for pleasure."[38] But that option seemed at least marginally less final than suicide. So the poet gathered his courage and,

Greek myths held that dolphins originated when a group of pirates tried to hold Dionysus, deity of fertility and wine, for ransom. The god turned himself into a lion and chased the pirates into the sea, then turned them into dolphins.

in Herodotus's words, "leapt into the sea, just as he was, with all his clothes on."[39] The ship moved on. Then, as Arion treaded water in an effort to stay afloat, a dolphin unexpectedly appeared. To the man's surprise, the creature maneuvered below him and carried him on its back to dry land.

A Need for the Neades?

There were also myths that explained the origins of many land animals. The rooster, for example, was said to have derived from a soldier who had guarded Ares, god of war. When that guard failed to awaken the deity early in the morning as instructed, Ares turned him into an *alektor*, or rooster, which by its nature had to announce the start of each new day.

Interestingly, the classical Greeks had a myth about the largest land creature of all before they even knew it existed. All through classical times, the residents of the Aegean island of Samos periodically unearthed huge bones from their soil. To explain this strange phenomenon, they cited a myth that claimed that giant beasts called Neades had once roamed the island. According to the fifth-century-BCE Samian writer Euagon, one day all of these beasts started loudly shrieking at the same time. That sound was so powerful, he said, it caused the ground to split open and swallow the Neades, whose bones remained there to be found centuries later.

Clearly, the Samians had a need for a story about animals like the Neades in order to explain the bones found in their local soil. But although it focused on that single island, the tale was widely known across the classical Greek world. The proof is that Greeks everywhere commonly employed the amusing adage "So-and-so shouts louder than the Neades!"[40]

Only toward the end of the classical period did the Greeks learn that beasts like the ones that had left their bones in Samos still existed. When the Macedonian Greek king Alexander the Great conquered much of western Asia in the late 300s BCE, he and his soldiers encountered elephants for the first time. In order to explain the existence of elephant skeletons in Samos, Greek thinkers now altered the myth about the Neades. The revised story claimed that the god Dionysus had fought a great battle in Samos against the Amazons, a mythical tribe of warrior women. Moreover, the big bones later discovered in Samian soil were none other than the remains of Dionysus's war elephants. (The reality is that early forms of elephants had lived in Samos millions of years before. But the Greeks did not yet know the world was that old.)

This rapid replacement of an ancient myth with a newer, more logical, story occurred after the rise of Greek science. It shows how

---

WORD ORIGINS

alektor

In ancient Greece: a rooster.

In modern life: alectromancy, a supposed method of foretelling the future by watching the way a rooster pecks at feed grain.

Close to Countless

The nymphs were by far the most numerous deities in Greek mythology, thought by the classical Greeks to be close to countless. In one manner or another, all were minor goddesses and female spirits inhabiting one niche or another of the natural world. According to legend, they maintained the earth's and heaven's wild beauty; ensured that flowers, trees, and other plants grew; helped nurture wild animals; and aided more powerful gods in preserving mountains, caves, clouds, beaches, and many other facets of nature.

The mythical origins of the nymphs varied widely. Some were daughters of Zeus. Others were offspring of various Titans, including Atlas, said to be father to three large clusters of nymphs—the Hesperides, Hyades, and Pleiades. In fact, almost all nymphs belonged to distinct groups. The Oceanids, for example, swam through the seas. Meanwhile, to name only a few other such groups, the Meliae oversaw ash trees and honey bees; the Oreads mountains; the Naiads lakes, rivers, and springs; the Dryades forests; the Epimelides grassy pastures and orchards; the Anthoussai flowers; the Nephelai rain clouds; and the Haliai seashores and coastal caverns.

Many Greeks made offerings to nymphs in hope of obtaining their favor. These sacrificial gifts most often consisted of milk, olive oil, goats, and lambs. People also erected shrines to their favorite nymphs, usually near streams, caves, and scenic forests. Greek and later Roman artists typically depicted nymphs as extremely attractive and frequently naked young women.

eager Greek scientists were to rationally, or reasonably, explain the workings of nature. They were willing to accept old myths as explanations of natural phenomena until newer evidence came along to refute them. As Adrienne Mayor points out, the newer myth "was a rational attempt to explain how in the world *elephants* came to be buried on an Aegean island."[41]

Chapter Five

From Mythology to Science

On one level, the ancient Greek tales that featured various natural phenomena proved to be, like all of the Greek myths, important surviving cultural artifacts. That is, these stories outlived the end of the ancient era and remained as charming relics of a long-dead people whose society was key to humanity's future. Indeed, modern historians agree that the classical Greeks' many ideas and accomplishments made Western civilization possible.

Yet those Greek myths about the weather, the heavenly bodies, animals and plants, and so forth also once possessed compelling scientific relevance and value. The late noted scholar T.B.L. Webster pointed out that these tales offered "an explanation of some natural process made in a period when such explanations were religious and magical rather than scientific."[42] In other words, the stories in question offered the equivalent of scientific explanations for various natural phenomena before the actual rise of science. Thus, the prescientific Greeks interpreted those explanations in religious terms, whereas the first scientists, who happened to be Greeks, sought to remove the gods and other mystical aspects from the equation. They searched for ways to explain such phenomena in what are today recognized as purely scientific terms.

For example, the earliest Greeks had been awestruck and fascinated by the blinding sun and its daily march across the sky. They had eagerly sought a way to explain it. But at the time the only effective tool they possessed for such speculation was religion. So they imagined that what their eyes saw as the sun was really the god Helios driving his shining chariot across the daytime sky. Only later did science show that the religious explanation was wrong. The sun proved to be a giant ball of hot gases that appears to cross the sky because Earth rotates on its axis once each day. Similarly, scientists showed that earthquakes were not caused by the deities Poseidon and Hephaestos, but rather by disturbances in Earth's slowly but constantly shifting crust.

The rise of science from the Greek thinkers on, therefore, can be seen as part of a gradual intellectual transition. It witnessed the steady replacement of an older, religion-based attempt to understand nature's workings with a newer, evidence-based approach to the same goal. In the words of respected researcher Arnold M. Katz, "Myth and science represent different ways of approaching a single objective: an understanding of the world around us. Both attempt to explain the creation of the world, the causes of natural phenomena, and even the origin of life."[43]

A System Governed by Laws

The scientific concepts introduced by the early Greek scientists did not suddenly and completely replace the older, myth-based system. The tales of a bronze sky-dome hovering a few miles above earth's surface and of Prometheus fashioning humans from mud persisted for centuries after the initial rise of science. For a long time it was mainly philosopher-scientists and other intellectuals who set aside the religion-based myths in favor of more natural explanations.

In contrast, all through Greece's classical era and even well past the end of Greco-Roman civilization in the 500s CE, most people, both inside and outside of Europe, were illiterate and uneducated. So they mostly held on to the belief that natural phenomena were the work of divine beings, magic, or both. This, according to scholar D.C. Lindberg, partially explains why "Greek mythology did not disappear but continued to flourish for centuries. Rather, it was the appearance

Ancient Greek myths sought to explain various natural phenomena such as the weather, the heavenly bodies, plants, and animals. Today the Southern Festoon butterfly (pictured) is widespread in Greece.

of new, philosophical modes of thought *alongside* or sometimes *mingled with* mythology."[44]

Yet despite Greek mythology's resilience and long-term survival, an understanding of how science eventually demoted those tales to mere entertaining folklore does begin with those early classical Greek philosopher-scientists. Modern experts use that compound term to describe them to stress that in their day, philosophy and science were not yet separate disciplines. Today the distinction between the two fields is fairly clear. Philosophy starts with observations and then proceeds to general speculations and arguments that need not be proved by evidence. In comparison, science involves observation and collecting evidence, followed by drawing conclusions directly from the evidence. Most early classical Greek thinkers mixed these two approaches in varying degrees.

Their general approach to understanding nature's wonders aside, these thinkers' greatest single achievement was to remove the gods and

Myth-Tellers' Corner: Euhemerus

Euhemerus, who was born in about 330 BCE and lived to be roughly seventy, was a Greek philosopher and prolific writer. His main works have not survived the ravages of time. But fragments of his writings were quoted in the *Library of History,* a long historical work by the first-century-BCE Greek historian Diodorus Siculus. Euhemerus was best known for his thesis that the gods of the ancient Greek myths had originally been ordinary humans whose reputations and powers had become exaggerated over time. In Diodorus's words:

> Certain of the gods, they say, are eternal and imperishable, such as the sun and the moon and the other stars of the heavens, and the winds as well and whatever else possesses a nature similar to theirs; for of each of these the genesis and duration are from everlasting to everlasting. But the other gods, we are told, were terrestrial [earthly] beings who attained to immortal honour and fame because of their benefactions to mankind, such as Heracles, Dionysus, Aristaeus, and the others who were like them. Regarding these terrestrial gods many and varying accounts have been handed down by the writers of history and of mythology; of the historians, Euhemerus, who composed the *Sacred History*, has written a special treatise about them, while, of the writers of myths, Homer and Hesiod and Orpheus and the others of their kind have invented rather monstrous stories about the gods.

Diodorus Siculus, *Library of History,* trans. C.H. Oldfather. In Theoi Greek Mythology. www.theoi.com.

other supernatural elements from their work. As modern scientists do, they viewed the heavenly bodies and other natural phenomena as material objects or forces that obeyed natural laws rather than the whims of gods. "It was assumed, for the first time in history," the late classical scholar Rex Warner said, "that the investigator was dealing with a universe that was a 'cosmos,' that is to say, an orderly system governed by laws which could be discovered by logical thought."[45]

Some Daring New Ideas

This was exactly how the first important Greek thinker, Thales, who flourished in the early 500s BCE, viewed nature. It was not by accident that he emerged in Miletus, a prosperous Greek city on the Aegean coast of what is now Turkey. An important center of trade, colonizing activity, and literature, Miletus had direct contacts with the older cultures of Egypt and Babylonia (now Iraq). Those peoples had long before made significant strides in mathematics and observing the heavens, and Thales freely borrowed some of their ideas. Unlike thinkers in the East, however, Thales rejected the age-old notion that the cosmos and nature operated through the wills of supernatural beings. He was the first known researcher who envisioned a natural order that worked via its own built-in, inanimate laws. Moreover, Thales proposed that that order contained a single, underlying natural principle he called the *physis*. The famous fourth-century-BCE Athenian scholar Aristotle said:

> Thales, the founder of this type of philosophy, declared the first-principle to be water, and for that reason he also held that Earth rests upon water. Probably the idea was suggested to him by the fact that everything contains moisture, and that heat itself is generated out of moisture. . . . He drew his notion also from the fact that the seeds of everything have a moist nature. And of course the first-principle of moist things is water.[46]

Thales, who lived in the early 500s BCE, was a Greek philosopher-scientist who sought to explain natural phenomena in scientific terms, rather than through myths. He theorized that all matter is a form or offshoot of water.

As it turned out, Thales's theory that all matter is a form or off-shoot of water was incorrect. Yet for its time it was extremely daring and forward thinking because it proposed a strictly physical basis for all of nature's phenomena. Partly inspired by him, other Greek thinkers employed the same bold approach.

Greek Medical Advances

Although floods, earthquakes, and volcanic eruptions killed a fair number of ancient Greeks over the centuries, the most deadly natural phenomenon was disease. Some of the early Greek scientists recognized this. They tried to eradicate sickness and alleviate the human suffering associated with it. As a result, medical advances were among the most important scientific achievements of Greece's classical era. Two highly respected medical schools appeared in that period—at Cnidus and Cos, both located northwest of the large eastern Aegean island of Rhodes. Modern experts agree that these schools developed research facilities, classroom instruction, and a program in which young men became apprentices to experienced physicians. Those physicians and their pupils took a solemn oath to aid the sick, care about the welfare of all people, and never kill or sexually abuse anyone. The first few generations of Greek physicians made medicine an authentic scientific discipline for the first time in human history. The most famous teacher at the Cos school was Hippocrates, who flourished in the late 400s BCE. In later ages he came to be called the "father" of medicine. Also, he, his fellow teachers, and their students generated numerous medical documents covering subjects that included surgery, anatomy, treatment by diet and drugs, and medical ethics. The most significant accomplishment made by both the Cos and Cnidus institutions was to keep medical knowledge separate from religious beliefs. This approach demonstrated that disease was truly a *natural* phenomenon, *not* a punishment sent by the gods.

One was Thales's own student, Anaximander (died circa 547 BCE). The sky was not a bronze dome beneath which Helios and Selene rode chariots and Zeus and other gods caused the planets to move, Anaximander argued. Instead, he stated, long ago a vast ring of fire exploded into existence. Over time it broke down into several smaller rings, which solidified into the sun, moon, and planets. This idea is remarkably similar to the modern view, in which the sun and planets coalesced from a large mass of hot, spinning gaseous materials. Anaximander also tackled the crucial mystery of the origins of life. Living creatures were not the handiwork of Prometheus and other deities, he insisted, but rather developed independently in the sea. Furthermore, over time the various species underwent gradual *amoebe*, or change. Some, like fish, remained in the sea, but others crawled out onto dry land and adapted themselves to their new surroundings, all concepts accepted by modern biologists.

> ## WORD ORIGINS
>
> ### *amoebe*
>
> In ancient Greece: change.
>
> In modern life: amoeba, a microscopic living thing that readily changes its shape.

Meanwhile, several other Greek thinkers continued the search for the *physis*. Of these efforts, most, as in Thales's case, led to inaccurate conclusions. One suggestion, however, strikingly foreshadowed the accepted modern concept of the basis of all matter. Two fifth-century-BCE Greeks—Leucippus and Democritus—proposed that everything is composed of tiny, microscopic particles that they called atoms.

Reduced to Mere Stories

For a while such ideas were known mostly to the members of a few small groups of intellectuals. Over time, however, as more and more Greeks became educated, scientific concepts became more widely known. Also, in the 300s BCE, toward the end of the classical period, science separated from philosophy and began to divide into the distinct branches familiar today, including biology, botany, astronomy, physics, and so forth.

Nevertheless, the traditional myths and their explanations for natural phenomena remained just as popular as they had been before. First, in spite of some real strides in education, most Greeks remained illiterate and clung to traditional, myth-based ideas for the workings of nature. Moreover, even most of the leading scholars of the day did not accept every new scientific proposal or advance. Aristotle was a notable example. He was both an intellectual giant in his own day and destined to remain an enormously influential authority in educated circles for more than two thousand years. Yet he rejected the atomic theory and stubbornly clung to the wrongheaded idea that Earth is the center of the cosmos.

Still another reason the old myths remained popular was that scholars and other writers continued to talk about and quote from them. One of these writers, Euhemerus, who lived in the late fourth century BCE, was particularly well known and influential. Like many other well-educated Greeks of his day, he held that the supernatural events in the myths had not actually occurred. Indeed, he claimed that the gods described in those tales were in reality just people—national rulers, military generals, and so forth. In his view, their images were grossly exaggerated over time until they morphed into godlike beings.

Euhemerus's ideas and writings remained widely popular in the centuries directly following the classical period. That had the effect of keeping the traditional myths alive and fashionable, even though he had debunked them. As the late Middlebury College scholar William Harris said in 1994, "The myths were reduced to a complicated system of formalized storytelling," and people never stopped enjoying hearing tall tales. Thus, he continues, it became

common to tell and retell the myths as imaginative stories, leaving historical origins aside, rather than trying to fathom an original meaning. A partial parallel may be seen in the fossilized Mother Goose stories which date from 18th century England. Children and their elders still enjoy telling and retelling the traditional tales about Jack and Jill, Humpty Dumpty, and the old lady who lived in a shoe, but most of us have no idea of what they mean.[47]

An Explosion of Popular Interest

Enjoyment of the Greek tales continues in a similar way. Harris adds, "Appreciation of most of the Greek myths is exactly of this nature. We know and retell and enjoy Greek mythology without having much idea of what it is really about."[48] Yet these stories still retain a certain value in and of themselves, he says, as they continue to capture new

Popular interest in Greek myths continues today, even though science has replaced them as a way to explain natural phenomena like the dramatic displays of light known as the aurora borealis (pictured), named after the Greek god of the north wind, Boreas.

audiences in each succeeding generation. This can be seen in the wide popularity of college professor Charles Kingsley's collection of Greek myths, *The Heroes*, first published in 1855 and still in print today; scholar and teacher Edith Hamilton's even more successful book of myths, which first appeared in 1940 and had its most recent reprinting in 2014; and Rick Riordan's hit series of adventure novels based on Greek mythology, which by 2015 had sold more than 30 million copies.

Notably, this tremendous modern explosion of popular interest in the Greek myths occurred even though science had long since replaced them as a way to explain the wonders of nature. After all, a long line of scientists—from Anaximander in the 500s BCE to Charles Darwin in 1859—demonstrated that Prometheus did not create the human race; rather, humans evolved naturally over time from less complex creatures. Also, it is a far cry from the bronze sky-dome floating a few miles up that the Greeks envisioned in 600 BCE to the 80 billion-trillion-miles-wide cosmos that astronomers estimated in 2015.

Having lost their "scientific" value, therefore, the Greek myths still thrive because they appeal so strongly to the human heart and innovative spirit. They entertain people and at the same time make them think about humanity's faults and virtues alike. Those stories "cover virtually all human experiences," Philip Mayerson points out, including "love, hate, war, tyranny, treachery, courage, fate," and many more. In this way, they "provide an endless source of inspiration for the creative imagination."[49]

Source Notes

Introduction: The Origins of Nature's Wonders

1. Ovid, *Metamorphoses*, trans. A.D. Melville, excerpted in Theoi Greek Mythology, "Phaethon." www.theoi.com.
2. Ovid, *Metamorphoses*, trans. Melville.
3. Ovid, *Metamorphoses*, trans. Melville.
4. Ovid, *Metamorphoses*, trans. Melville.
5. Adrienne Mayor, *The First Fossil Hunters: Paleontology in Greek and Roman Times*. Princeton, NJ: Princeton University Press, 2000, p. 193.
6. Philip Mayerson, *Classical Mythology in Literature, Art, and Music*. Newburyport, MA: Pullins, 2001, p. 280.

Chapter One: Weather and Natural Disasters

7. Samantha-Rae Tuthill, "Weather and Ancient Religion: Greek Mythology," AccuWeather.com, August 20, 2012. www.accu weather.com.
8. Stewart Perowne, introduction to *The Illustrated Dictionary of Greek and Roman Mythology*, by Michael Stapleton. New York: Bedrick, 1986, p. 6.
9. Pseudo-Apollodorus, *Bibliotheca*, trans. Keith Aldrich, excerpted in Theoi Greek Mythology, "Gigantes." www.theoi.com.
10. Pseudo-Apollodorus, *Bibliotheca*.
11. Thomas Taylor, trans., "Orphic Hymn 19 to Zeus of Lightning," in Theoi Greek Mythology, "Zeus." www.theoi.com.
12. Taylor, "Orphic Hymn 18 to Zeus of Thunder."
13. Homer, *Odyssey*. Book 10, lines 4–5, trans. Don Nardo.
14. Homer, *Odyssey*, Book 10, lines 6–26, trans. Don Nardo.
15. Herodotus, *Histories*, trans. Aubrey de Sélincourt. New York: Pen-

guin, 1996, p. 403.

16. Clinton Corcoran, "The Slow Boat from Delos, or Socrates' Ship Comes In?," *Nautilus*, Spring 2010, p. 33.

17. Philostratus the Elder, *Imagines*, trans. Arthur Fairbanks, excerpted in Theoi Greek Mythology, "Enkelados." www.theoi.com.

18. Quoted in Waldo E. Sweet, ed., *Sport and Recreation in Ancient Greece: A Sourcebook with Translations*. New York: Oxford University Press, 1987, p. 158.

19. Richard Buxton, *Myths and Tragedies in Their Ancient Greek Contexts*. New York: Oxford University Press, 2013, p. 214.

20. Buxton, *Myths and Tragedies in Their Ancient Greek Contexts*, p. 214.

Chapter Two: The Celestial Sphere

21. *Homeric Hymn to Selene*, in *Hesiod, The Homeric Hymns, and Homerica*, trans. H.G. Evelyn-White. Cambridge, MA: Harvard University Press, 1964, pp. 459, 461.

22. Aratus of Soli, *Phenomena*, trans. G.R. Mair, in Theoi Greek Mythology. www.theoi.com.

23. Aratus of Soli, *Phenomena*.

24. Pseudo-Hyginus, *Astronomica*, trans. Mary Grant, excerpted in Theoi Greek Mythology, "Aigipan." www.theoi.com.

25. *Homeric Hymn to the Dioscuri*, in *Hesiod, The Homeric Hymns, and Homerica*, trans. H.G. Evelyn-White. Cambridge, MA: Harvard University Press, 1964, p. 463.

26. Ovid, *Metamorphoses*, trans. Mary M. Innes. London: Penguin, 2006, p. 60.

Chapter Three: Fire and the Seasons

27. Aeschylus, *Prometheus Bound*, in *Aeschylus: Prometheus Bound, the Suppliants, Seven Against Thebes, the Persians*, trans. Philip Vellacott. Baltimore: Penguin, 1961, p. 34.

28. Aeschylus, *Prometheus Bound*, p. 24.

29. Lesley Adkins and Roy A. Adkins, *Handbook to Life in Ancient Greece*. New York: Facts On File, 2005, p. 346.

30. *Homeric Hymn to Demeter*, in *Hesiod, The Homeric Hymns, and Homerica*, trans. H.G. Evelyn-White. Cambridge, MA: Harvard

University Press, 1964, p. 293.

31. *Homeric Hymn to Demeter*, in *Hesiod, The Homeric Hymns, and Homerica*, p. 313.
32. *Homeric Hymn to Demeter*, in *Hesiod, The Homeric Hymns, and Homerica*, p. 325.

Chapter Four: Plants and Animals

33. Ovid, *Metamorphoses*, trans. Innes, p. 229.
34. Ovid, *Metamorphoses*, trans. Innes, p. 230.
35. Ovid, *Metamorphoses*, trans. Innes, p. 230.
36. Edith Hamilton, *The Greek Way*. New York: Norton, 1993, p. 24.
37. Ovid, *Metamorphoses*, trans. Innes, p. 144.
38. Robin Lane Fox, *Traveling Heroes: Greeks and Their Myths in the Age of Homer*. New York: Vintage, 2010, p. 170.
39. Herodotus, *Histories*, p. 49.
40. Quoted in Mayor, *The First Fossil Hunters*, p. 57.
41. Mayor, *The First Fossil Hunters*, p. 55.

Chapter Five: From Mythology to Science

42. Quoted in Carlos Paradas, "Basic Aspects of the Greek Myths," Greek Mythology Link. www.maicar.com.
43. Arnold M. Katz, "Emergence of Scientific Explanations of Nature in Ancient Greece," *Circulation*, 1995. http://circ.ahajournals.org.
44. D.C. Lindberg, *The Beginnings of Western Science*. Chicago: University of Chicago Press, 1992, p. 25.
45. Rex Warner, *The Greek Philosophers*. New York: New American Library, 1958, pp. 9–10.
46. Aristotle, *Metaphysics*, excerpted in Philip Wheelwright, trans. and ed., *The Presocratics*. New York: Macmillan, 1966, pp. 46–47.
47. William Harris, "Euhemerism: The Greek Myths," Humanities and the Liberal Arts. http://community.middlebury.edu.
48. Harris, "Euhemerism."
49. Mayerson, *Classical Mythology in Literature, Art, and Music*, p. 2.

For Further Research

Books

Marc Aronson and Adrienne Mayor, *The Griffin and the Dinosaur: How Adrienne Mayor Discovered a Fascinating Link Between Myth and Science*. Washington, DC: National Geographic, 2014.

Arthur Cotterel, *The Illustrated A–Z of Classic Mythology*. Leicester, England: Lorenz, 2014.

David E. Falkner, *The Mythology of the Night Sky: An Amateur Astronomer's Guide to the Ancient Greek and Roman Legends*. New York: Springer, 2011.

Edith Hamilton, *Mythology*. New York: Grand Central, 2011.

Glen Huser, *Time for Flowers, Time for Snow: A Retelling of the Legend of Demeter and Persephone*. Vancouver, BC: Tradewind, 2013.

Tom Kindley, *Heroes of the Night Sky: The Greek Myths Behind the Constellations*. London: Cicada, 2016.

Charles Kingsley, *The Heroes*. Santa Barbara, CA: Mission Audio, 2011.

Mark P.O. Morford and Robert J. Lenardon, *Classical Mythology*. New York: Oxford University Press, 2010.

Donna Jo Napoli, *Treasury of Greek Mythology: Classic Stories of Gods, Goddesses, Heroes, and Monsters*. New York: National Geographic, 2011.

George O'Conner, *Zeus, King of the Gods*. New York: First Second, 2010.

Internet Sources

Mike Belmont, "The Greek God Hephaestus." Gods and Monsters, 2015. www.gods-and-monsters.com/greek-god-hephaestus.html.

N.S. Gill, "Prometheus: Fire Bringer and Philanthropist," About.com, 2015. http://ancienthistory.about.com/cs/grecoromanmyth1/a/prometheus.htm.

Livius.org, "The Great Flood: The Greco-Roman Story," 2007. www.livius.org/fa-fn/flood/flood4.html.

Pedro Media-Landa, "Myths and Legends on Natural Disasters: Making Sense of Our World," Yale–New Haven Teachers Institute, 2015. www.yale.edu/ynhti/curriculum/units/2007/4/07.04.13.x.html#d.

Skywise Unlimited, "Greek Mythology and the Constellations." www.wwu.edu/depts/skywise/greekmyth.html.

Websites

Greek Mythology Link (www.maicar.com/GML/index.html). This well-thought-out site has a biographical dictionary with more than six thousand entries and some forty-five hundred photos, drawings, and other images.

Medea's Lair: Tales of Greek Mythology (www.medeaslair.net/myths.html). The authors of this site do a nice job of retelling the old myths, which are grouped into categories that include "Men and Heroes," "Tales of Love and Loss," and "Giants and Beasts."

Mythweb Encyclopedia of Greek Mythology (www.mythweb.com/encyc). This website provides a lot of useful information about both major and minor Greek mythological characters.

Theoi Greek Mythology (www.theoi.com). This is the most comprehensive and reliable general website about Greek mythology on the Internet. It features hundreds of separate pages filled with detailed, accurate information, as well as numerous primary sources.

Index

Picture Credits

About the Author

Classical historian Don Nardo has written numerous acclaimed volumes about ancient civilizations and peoples. They include more than a dozen overviews of the mythologies of the Sumerians, Babylonians, Egyptians, Greeks, Romans, Persians, and others. Nardo also composes and arranges orchestral music. He lives with his wife, Christine, in Massachusetts.